AN ALBUM OF
MARTIN LUTHER KING, JR.

Dr. Martin Luther King, Jr., hugs his wife, Coretta, at a news conference following the announcement that he was awarded the Nobel Peace Prize, 1964. (UNITED PRESS INTERNATIONAL)

AN ALBUM OF
MARTIN LUTHER KING, JR.

by JEANNE A. ROWE

Franklin Watts, Inc.
575 Lexington Avenue
New York, N.Y. 10022

Cover photo:
Dr. Martin Luther King, Jr., addressing the tremendous crowd who came to Washington, D.C., on August 28, 1963, for the March on Washington. (PICTORIAL PARADE)

SBN 531 01509-2

Copyright © 1970 by Franklin Watts, Inc.
Library of Congress Catalog Card Number: 73-110474
Printed in the United States of America

1 2 3 4 5

CONTENTS

Dr. Martin Luther King, Jr. (1929–68)

MARTIN LUTHER KING, JR.

Dr. Martin Luther King, Jr., dedicated his life to the crusade for racial equality. To millions of black Americans, he was the country's foremost civil rights leader. He urged his people to be proud of their race. He asked them to stand up for their rights. He led them in nonviolent demonstrations against the evils of hatred and segregation. He was a prophet of peace. Dr. King believed in the basic goodness of man and in the philosophy of nonviolence. It was his hope and dream that nonviolent protest action would create an America where all men might truly be equal. His efforts brought him worldwide fame, and death at an early age.

EARLY LIFE

Martin Luther King, Jr., was born in Atlanta, Georgia, on January 15, 1929. The poverty that blighted the lives of so many other black Americans was not part of his growing up. He lived in Auburn, the section of Atlanta where many successful black business and professional men made their homes. His close relatives were active in the community. His maternal grandfather, A. D. Williams, was one of the first leaders of the Georgia National Association for the Advancement of Colored People, the NAACP. Williams was involved in a boycott of the Atlanta *Georgian*, a newspaper that had insulted black voters. A "boycott" means to refuse to buy, sell, or use a product or service. The boycott by six thousand blacks forced the *Georgian* out of business. Martin's father, the Reverend Martin Luther King, Sr., led the fight for equal salaries for black teachers in Atlanta, and for the abolition in the Atlanta courthouse of separate, or Jim Crow, elevators for blacks. He also taught his son how to preach to a congregation.

Martin (seated, right)
and his family, in 1939.
(MRS. MARTIN LUTHER KING, SR.)

Reverend Martin Luther King, Sr., talks to housing demonstrators in Boston in 1968. Many men of the King family were ministers, and all were active in the fight for civil rights. (UNITED PRESS INTERNATIONAL)

Martin Luther King, Jr., did not suffer directly from poverty as a child, but he did experience discrimination and segregation. And it made him angry. He could not understand why two white boys across the street would not play with him. He hated the Jim Crow laws that separated white people from black people in theaters, trains, buses, and other public places and conveyances. These humiliations remained in the back of his mind, and he hoped that when he was older he would be able to fight against them.

Martin was a very good student at school and worked hard at his studies. He skipped the ninth and twelfth grades of high school and at the age of fifteen entered Morehouse College in Atlanta. At first Martin thought he would study medicine or law. But by the time he reached his junior year he decided that he could do more for his people as a minister, and in 1948 he began his studies at Crozer Theological Seminary in Chester, Pennsylvania.

At the Crozer Theological Seminary, Martin Luther King, one of six black students in a student body of about a hundred, was graduated first in his class and elected president of the student body. He was named the seminary's outstanding student and won a fellowship to study for a doctorate degree. He decided to do his graduate work at Boston University. While studying in Boston, he met Coretta Scott, a graduate of Antioch College and a voice student at the New England Conservatory of Music. He married her in 1953, and a year later they moved to Montgomery, Alabama, where the Dexter Avenue Baptist Church of Montgomery had offered him his first parish assignment. From the pulpit King urged his people to join the civil rights fight and to register to vote. In 1955 he finished his thesis for the Ph.D. degree at Boston University and earned the title of doctor.

Dexter Avenue Baptist Church, Montgomery, Alabama. (WIDE WORLD PHOTOS)

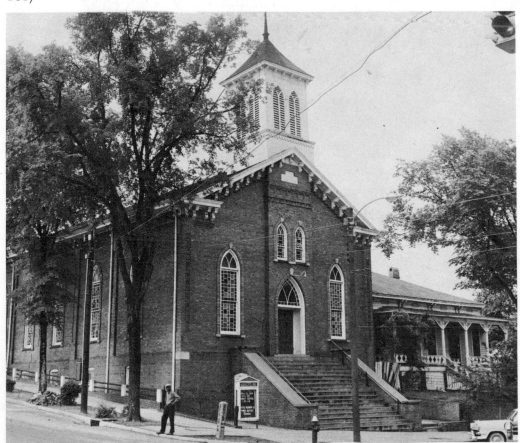

Mrs. King at the piano with the King children: (left to right) Yolanda, Bernice, Dexter, and Martin III. Mrs. King was a professional singer and often sang at civil rights meetings. (UNITED PRESS INTERNATIONAL)

Dr. King's home in Montgomery, Alabama. (WIDE WORLD PHOTOS)

Dr. Martin Luther King holds his sons Martin Luther III (left) and Dexter in his arms in his old home in Atlanta, Georgia, in 1964. On the wall is a portrait of Gandhi, the Indian leader who inspired Dr. King in his work. (FRANK DANDRIDGE, PIX)

'At Crozer Theological Seminary, King discovered the nonviolent philosophy of Mahatma Gandhi, the Indian nationalist who had led his countrymen in their successful struggle against British rule of their homeland. Gandhi had drawn some of his ideas from the writings of Henry David Thoreau, the nineteenth-century American philosopher and naturalist. Thoreau's essay *Civil Disobedience* helped inspire Gandhi to urge his people to use the method of noncooperation in their struggle for freedom. Instead of arming his people, Gandhi urged them to strike British factories, to boycott British products, and to march in demonstrations of protest. The Indians won their independence with a minimum of bloodshed. King believed that Gandhi's nonviolent method of protest would be useful in a minority's fight against oppression by a majority. (Black people made up only 10 percent of America's population.)

11

Mahatma Gandhi (right) in 1946 with Jawaharlal Nehru, newly elected president of the All-India Congress. Nehru was later to become prime minister of an independent India. Dr. King used Gandhi's methods of nonviolence and noncooperation in his battle for equal rights for black Americans. (UNITED PRESS INTERNATIONAL)

In India in 1930 Gandhi's followers staged many incidents of noncooperation with British authorities. This line of strikers lay in front of the gate of their factory to prevent strikebreakers from entering. (UNITED PRESS INTERNATIONAL)

12

THE MONTGOMERY STORY

Martin Luther King, Jr., was not yet twenty-seven years old when an event occurred in Montgomery, Alabama, that was to change his life and raise him to world prominence. On December 1, 1955, Mrs. Rosa Parks, a black seamstress, boarded a Montgomery public bus and took a seat. She had been shopping all day and was very tired. Soon all the seats in the bus were filled. As the bus began to pick up more people along the way, the driver told Negro passengers to give their seats to white passengers. The driver told Mrs. Parks to get up and give her seat to a white man who had just entered. When Mrs. Parks refused to leave her seat, she was arrested. Negro leaders in the city decided to stage a one-day bus boycott in protest.

Mrs. Rosa Parks and Dr. Martin Luther King, Jr., in 1965. (UNITED PRESS INTERNATIONAL)

Dr. Martin Luther King, Jr., speaks to an overflow crowd at the Holt St. Baptist Church in Montgomery, Alabama, on March 22, 1956. (WIDE WORLD PHOTOS)

On the morning of the boycott, Martin Luther King, Jr., and his wife rushed to the window to see if anybody was riding the buses. Every bus that passed King's house that day was almost completely empty. The boycott was 99 percent effective. When city leaders still refused to discuss the desegregation of city buses with the Negro community, the boycott continued. Dr. King was chosen president of the Montgomery Improvement Association, an organization formed to run the boycott. For 381 more days Negroes refused to ride the Montgomery City Line buses. They walked, they rode in wagons drawn by mules and horses, they organized a car pool. They were determined to sacrifice for their dignity. From pulpits throughout the city King urged his people to follow Gandhi's philosophy of nonviolent struggle. His talents as a leader and a speaker were first noted in this fight for freedom.

The boycott continued and the car pool grew to a fleet of three hundred. Segregationists struck back. They arrested King on a fake charge. Then four days later a bomb was thrown on the porch of his home. King, who had not been home at the time, arrived fifteen minutes later to find an outraged crowd of blacks armed with guns and rocks. He stood on his porch with frightened city officials and urged his people not to use violence. He said they must continue the boycott without returning evil for evil. Later, King was arrested again. Finally the Supreme Court of the United States ruled that bus segregation in Alabama was unconstitutional. Montgomery's buses were integrated. The blacks had won. They now had greater self-respect and they had a leader.

Dr. Martin Luther King, Jr., speaks from the porch of his home after it was damaged by a bomb during the Montgomery bus boycott. Standing next to him are (left to right) Montgomery's fire chief, mayor (in uniform), and police chief. King urged an angry black community to remain calm. (UNITED PRESS INTERNATIONAL)

In 1956, after 382 days of boycott, Montgomery's blacks were boarding newly integrated buses. (WIDE WORLD PHOTOS)

Dr. Martin Luther King, Jr., leader of the Montgomery bus boycott, rides in the front of a Montgomery bus after the Supreme Court's decision that bus segregation in Alabama is unconstitutional. (UNITED PRESS INTERNATIONAL)

Dr. King is brought to the jailhouse in Montgomery, Alabama, in 1958. He was charged with loitering, and then released. (CHARLES MOORE, BLACK STAR)

After the Montgomery triumph, black people throughout the nation began to be aware of young Dr. King and his nonviolent methods of protest. He became president of a new organization — the Southern Christian Leadership Conference (SCLC) — an organization of church groups devoted to social action in behalf of equality for black people. King moved to Atlanta, Georgia, and gave up his pastorship of the Dexter Avenue Church. Because he had dared to speak out forcefully against segregation, he was now in great danger. Sometimes the danger came from white officials who arrested him on trumped-up charges and treated him harshly. Sometimes it came from the Ku Klux Klan, the Southern terrorist group that threatened blacks with violence. In 1958, in a Harlem department store, King was autographing *Stride Toward Freedom*, a book about the Montgomery boycott, when a deranged black woman stabbed him. King narrowly escaped death.

17

In 1960 Dr. King, with his two-year-old son, Martin Luther III, found a charred cross which the Ku Klux Klan had burned on his front lawn. Dr. King and his family lived constantly under the threat of violence. (UNITED PRESS INTERNATIONAL)

An attending physician stands at the bedside of Dr. Martin Luther King, Jr., in Harlem Hospital after a three-hour emergency operation to remove a knife from his chest. King was stabbed by a black woman while he was autographing copies of his book. (UNITED PRESS INTERNATIONAL)

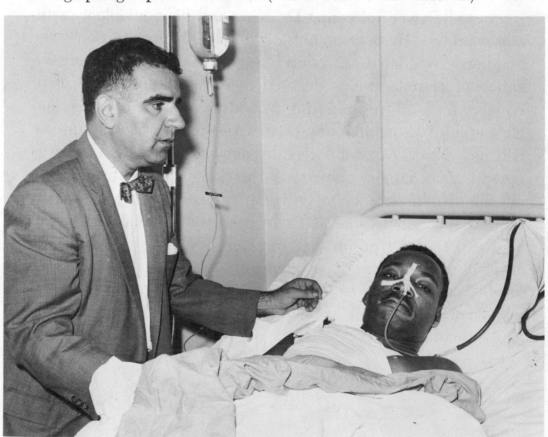

While King and SCLC were still making plans, the fight for civil rights was speeded up by the spontaneous action of four black college students. One afternoon in February, 1960, the students went into a five-and-dime store in Greensboro, North Carolina, and sat down at a lunch counter. In Greensboro, seats at lunch counters were for whites only. That day, and for many days thereafter, the students and their friends sat down at lunch counters, quietly waiting to be served. The idea spread rapidly. More and more students staged sit-ins. King joined a sit-in at Rich's Department Store in Atlanta. He was arrested and jailed. Presidential candidate John F. Kennedy phoned Mrs. King to express his concern for Dr. King. Shortly after, King was set free. The call was credited with turning the nation's black vote toward Kennedy in the 1960 election.

Black students sit in to protest segregation at a lunch counter in Chattanooga, Tennessee, in 1960. (UNITED PRESS INTERNATIONAL)

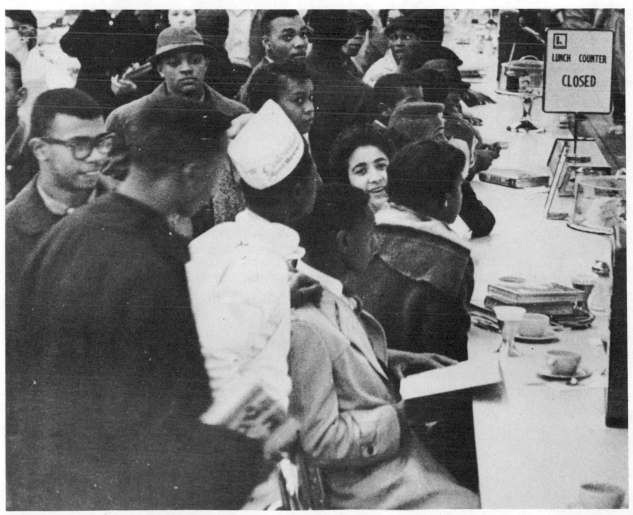

Freedom Riders are driven from their bus by a fire started by segregation-ists. (UNITED PRESS INTERNATIONAL)

In May, 1961, the civil rights movement attacked segregation on a new front. The Congress of Racial Equality (CORE), a Northern-based civil rights organization, sent integrated buses to cities throughout the South to test the long-standing court orders bar-ring segregation in interstate transportation. These interracial trips became known as the Freedom Rides. When the Freedom Ride buses reached the terminals of several Southern cities, they were bombed and burned by racists. The Freedom Riders were badly beaten and stoned. Dr. King rushed to Montgomery, Ala-bama, the scene of one assault on the Freedom Riders, to give courage to the black community. They gathered to hear him speak at the First Baptist Church. Outside the church an angry mob of segregationists threatened violence. Finally, the gover-nor of Alabama declared martial law and sent National Guards-men to the troubled spot. A few days later King was asked to be the spokesman of a committee consisting of all the civil rights groups involved in the Freedom Rides.

ALBANY, GEORGIA

After the Freedom Rides, Dr. King began organizing the community of Albany, Georgia, for nonviolent struggle. He wanted Albany to end the segregation of libraries and recreational facilities, to hire black policemen and busmen, and to set up an interracial council. Seventy-five Protestant, Jewish, and Catholic religious leaders came down to Albany at King's request to join him in a prayer vigil for racial justice. Although their arrest after a march to the city hall aroused some concern in Northern newspapers, the federal government did not use its influence with city officials. King organized mass marches and was arrested three times for doing so. The police in Albany abstained from violence. King's efforts did not succeed in changing any of Albany's segregation practices.

Policemen in Albany, Georgia, carry a teen-age demonstrator out of the Albany Carnegie Library. About fifteen young blacks went into the library to pray and sing in protest against segregation. (UNITED PRESS INTERNATIONAL)

More and more religious leaders from the North joined the civil rights movement after 1960. In 1962 a group of white and black religious leaders of various faiths responded with raised hands in an Albany, Georgia, church when Dr. King asked if they would be "willing to go to jail for our cause." Minutes later, after marching to the city hall, the religious leaders were arrested and jailed. (UNITED PRESS INTERNATIONAL)

Dr. Martin Luther King, Jr. (left, front) and the Reverend Ralph Abernathy (right) talk to young men in an Albany, Georgia, poolroom in 1962. King and his aide discussed the philosophy of nonviolent protest with them and asked them to join the civil rights movement. (UNITED PRESS INTERNATIONAL)

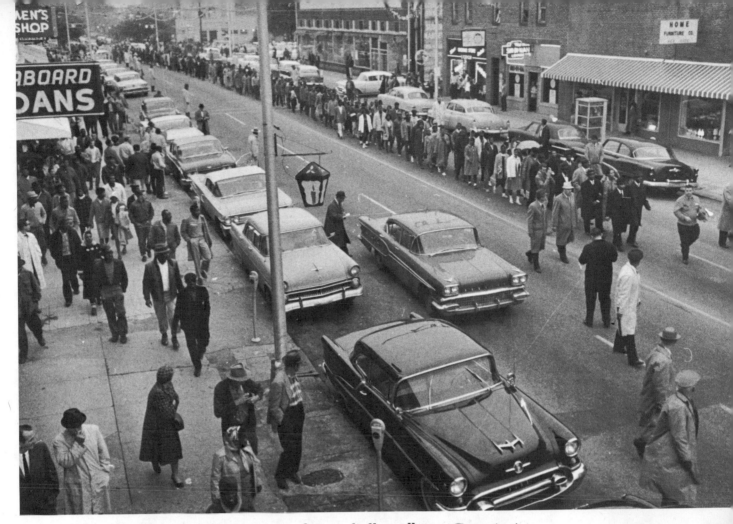

Dr. Martin Luther King leads a march on the city hall in Albany, Georgia, in 1961. (UNITED PRESS INTERNATIONAL)

Albany, Georgia, police chief, Laurie Pritchett (right), tells Dr. Martin Luther King and Dr. W. G. Anderson that they are under arrest since they cannot show a parade permit, December 16, 1961. (UNITED PRESS INTERNATIONAL)

23

BIRMINGHAM, ALABAMA

In 1962, the Southern Christian Leadership Conference decided that the next move for civil rights should take place in Birmingham, Alabama, the largest industrial city in the South. At that time, Birmingham was one of the most segregated cities in America. If segregation could be defeated in Birmingham, Dr. King felt, then perhaps it could also be defeated throughout all of America. The first demonstrations against Birmingham's racial caste system took place in downtown Birmingham in 1963, one hundred years after the Emancipation Proclamation freed the slaves. Small groups of blacks sat in at downtown lunch counters, libraries, and drugstores. In the evenings Dr. King spoke at church meetings. The entire black community turned out to hear him discuss the philosophy and methods of nonviolence.

During the Birmingham civil rights campaign, much of Dr. King's time was spent raising money for the movement. He addresses a crowd at St. Paul's Episcopal Church in Cleveland, Ohio, May, 1963. (UNITED PRESS INTERNATIONAL)

"Bull" Connor, commissioner of public safety of Birmingham, Alabama, became a symbol of police brutality in 1963 when he ordered police to use fire hoses and dogs on nonviolent demonstrators. (UNITED PRESS INTERNATIONAL)

Day after day in April, 1963, more and more black men and women joined the demonstrations in downtown Birmingham. They kneeled in at churches and sat in at the public library. They marched through the downtown business section and boycotted and picketed downtown stores. "Bull" Connor, Birmingham's commissioner of public safety, refused to discuss the issues with Dr. King and other civil rights leaders. Connor ordered the police to arrest the demonstrators. They went to jail by the hundreds. On Good Friday, April 12, Dr. King led a march through downtown Birmingham, and was arrested. Nobody — not even his lawyer or his wife — was allowed to see him for twenty-four hours. Coretta King was worried and telephoned President Kennedy for help. The President's brother Attorney General Robert Kennedy telephoned Birmingham officials and shortly thereafter Dr. King was allowed to speak with his wife.

A six-year-old black girl was arrested in Birmingham, Alabama, on May 2, 1963. Over 450 schoolchildren were arrested on the same day in demonstrations organized by Dr. King. (WIDE WORLD PHOTOS)

In a nine-thousand-word letter to America from his Birmingham jail cell, Dr. King told the nation that black Americans would no longer stand by and wait for freedom to be given to them, but would wage a persistent battle to achieve it for themselves. Shortly after his letter Dr. King posted bond and left jail. The Birmingham campaign had slackened, and his leadership was badly needed. Then black children urged Dr. King to let them join the fight. This was a very difficult decision for him to make. Would he be accused of using children to fight an adult battle? Dr. King felt that black children were hurt most by the evils of segregation, and he believed that they would have the most to gain from its defeat. So he agreed to let them join the Birmingham campaign. They joined in numbers beyond his expectations. Day after day, groups of young black students, from ages six to sixteen, marched on downtown Birmingham. Many were arrested and sent to jail.

Over three thousand blacks were jailed in the Birmingham demonstrations in 1963. The jails were always filled, and city officials did not know where to put additional demonstrators. Hundreds of black teen-age girls who had been arrested were put in a building at the state fairgrounds. (WIDE WORLD PHOTOS)

During the Birmingham crisis Dr. King called on the national Negro community for support. Floyd Patterson (left), former heavyweight champion, and Jackie Robinson (right), former Dodgers' baseball player, join Dr. Martin Luther King and his chief aide, Ralph Abernathy, at a rally in a Birmingham church, on May 13, 1963. (UNITED PRESS INTERNATIONAL)

27

On Tuesday, May 7, twenty-five hundred black people poured out of a Birmingham church and began marching downtown to protest continued segregation in the city. Public Safety Commissioner "Bull" Connor became furious, and ordered the police to break up the demonstration. Television viewers throughout the nation were shocked when they saw unarmed men, women, and children swept down the streets by the powerful blast of water from fire hoses. They saw snarling police dogs threaten defenseless people and they saw the police become violent as they clubbed their way into crowds. They saw fallen demonstrators harshly dragged to patrol wagons. Not only Americans were horrified by what was happening in Birmingham; the news traveled around the entire world. National and international public opinion was a new force Birmingham's officials had to contend with.

A fire hose is turned on full force against black demonstrators in Birmingham, Alabama, in 1963. (WIDE WORLD PHOTOS)

Police dogs in Birmingham, Alabama, tear the clothing of black demonstrators during the Birmingham campaign in May, 1963. (CHARLES MOORE, BLACK STAR)

Americans were very unhappy about the police brutality they witnessed in Birmingham. Their nation claimed a strong devotion to democracy and decency, and such outbursts of official violence could not be tolerated. Birmingham's officials sensed the mood of the country. They finally realized that Dr. King's movement could not be stopped and they met with him. They agreed to bring about some desegregation and to set up an interracial council. Many white southerners refused to accept the agreement peacefully. The Gaston Motel — headquarters of the integrationists — and the home of Dr. King's brother were dynamited after a Ku Klux Klan meeting on May 11. Blacks were furious and rampaged through the streets. King, who had been in Atlanta, returned to Birmingham to calm his followers. Peace came slowly to the city even after President Kennedy announced that the federal government would call up the Alabama National Guard if there was any further trouble in Birmingham.

Dr. King, together with Reverend Abernathy, holds a press conference on April 9 to tell the people that they are negotiating with Birmingham's city officials to end racial strife. (UNITED PRESS INTERNATIONAL)

On May 11, the home of the Reverend A. D. King, the brother of Dr. Martin Luther King, was dynamited in Birmingham, Alabama. A series of bombings shook Birmingham soon after the settlement in 1963. (WIDE WORLD PHOTOS)

AFTER BIRMINGHAM

Birmingham was a triumph for Dr. King. After Birmingham he was acknowledged to be the foremost American in the fight for civil rights. At this time Dr. King discussed his ideas about nonviolence in his books *Strength to Love* and *Why We Can't Wait*. He traveled throughout the country, speaking to large audiences and leading protest demonstrations. He led over 125,000 people on a freedom march in Detroit, Michigan. Black and white people joined peaceful protest marches in over eight hundred American cities. Racists reacted to these demonstrations with violence. In Jackson, Mississippi, Medgar W. Evers, the Mississippi field secretary of the NAACP, was shot to death as he stepped out of an automobile in the driveway of his home. Freedom walker William Moore was killed in Alabama. Four little black girls died when a dynamite blast went off during Sunday School in a Birmingham, Alabama, church.

Many Americans were horrified by this outburst of violence, and they called for legislative action.

Shocked friends and relatives file past the casket of slain civil rights leader Medgar Evers in 1963. (UNITED PRESS INTERNATIONAL)

Dr. Martin Luther King (left) and Roy Wilkins (middle) lead three thousand black marchers through downtown Jackson, Mississippi, after the funeral of slain civil rights leader Medgar Evers. (UNITED PRESS INTERNATIONAL)

Four little black girls were killed when a bomb exploded at the Sixteenth Street Baptist Church in Birmingham, Alabama, on September 15, 1963. The force of the blast was so strong that the windows of the church were blown out and cars outside were damaged. (UNITED PRESS INTERNATIONAL)

The funeral for four young black girls killed when a bomb exploded at the Sixteenth Street Baptist Church in Birmingham, Alabama. (UNITED PRESS INTERNATIONAL)

Dr. Martin Luther King, Jr., dressed in black robes, with a beam of sunlight streaming through the windows behind him, conducts the funeral service for four black girls killed in a bomb explosion in a Birmingham church, in 1963. (UNITED PRESS INTERNATIONAL)

MARCH ON WASHINGTON

The largest demonstration ever to take place in America occurred in Washington, D.C., on August 28, 1963. The demonstration was organized to lend support to President Kennedy's proposed civil rights bill and to urge the formation of a desegregated society. The demonstration was organized by civil rights groups — NAACP, CORE, SCLC, SNCC, and others — and labor, religious, business, and entertainment organizations. Over 200,000 black and white people of all ages, from all parts of America, poured into Washington to march from the Washington Monument to the Lincoln Memorial. They came by plane, car, bus, and train. They came to support black demands for better job opportunities, for integrated schools and public facilities, and for greater representation on public committees.

Leaders of six national Negro organizations meet at a New York hotel in July, 1963, to plan the march in support of President Kennedy's civil rights legislation. Left to right: John Lewis, chairman of the Student Nonviolent Co-ordinating Committee (SNCC); Whitney Young, Jr., director of the National Urban League; A. Phillip Randolph, president of the National Negro Labor Congress; Dr. Martin Luther King, Jr., president of the Southern Christian Leadership Council; James Farmer, national director of the Congress of Racial Equality (CORE); and Roy Wilkins, executive secretary of the National Association for the Advancement of Colored People (NAACP). (UNITED PRESS INTERNATIONAL)

Freedom marchers from Pennsylvania arrive at Washington, D.C.'s Union Station, in 1963, to take part in the March on Washington for Jobs and Freedom. (CHARLES MOORE, BLACK STAR)

Leaders of the March on Washington lock arms as they move along Constitution Avenue in Washington, D.C., in 1963. Dr. Martin Luther King is fourth from the left. (UNITED PRESS INTERNATIONAL)

Dr. Martin Luther King, Jr., gives his "I Have a Dream" speech to 200,000 black and white Americans who came to Washington, D.C., on August 28, 1963, for the March on Washington. (PICTORIAL PARADE, INC.)

For three hours, 200,000 marchers, and millions of television viewers at home throughout the country, listened to speakers demand passage of the civil rights bill. The speech they remember most was the one given by Dr. Martin Luther King, Jr. Dr. King's speeches were always magnetic. He had been able to voice the black battle cry for human dignity more strongly than anyone else. On this day, Dr. King's vibrant baritone voice rang out with his dream for a better America. He wished for a better life for his children and for all of the children of the world. He prayed that injustice and racism would disappear from the face of the earth so that all men might truly become brothers.

The March on Washington as seen from the inside of the Lincoln Memorial on August 28, 1963. People numbering 200,000 fill the area between the Lincoln Memorial and the Washington Monument to hear Dr. King speak, one hundred years after Lincoln's Emancipation Proclamation. (UNITED PRESS INTERNATIONAL)

President Kennedy, meets with civil rights leaders following the March on Washington. Left to right (front row): Whitney Young (National Urban League); Dr. Martin Luther King, Jr. (Southern Leadership Conference); Rabbi Joachim Prinz (Chairman, American Jewish Congress); A. Phillip Randolph (March director); President Kennedy; Walter Reuther (Vice-President, AFL-CIO); Roy Wilkins (NAACP). (UNITED PRESS INTERNATIONAL)

In 1963, after the March on Washington, many groups throughout the nation used King's methods of nonviolent protest to fight for integration and equal employment. Demonstrators in Brooklyn, New York, chain themselves together to protest job discrimination in the construction of a hospital. (UNITED PRESS INTERNATIONAL)

Protesters sing freedom songs in a demonstration against a segregated amusement park in Baltimore, Maryland, in 1963. (UNITED PRESS INTERNATIONAL)

After having signed the Civil Rights Act of 1964 in a White House ceremony on July 2, President Johnson shakes hands with Dr. Martin Luther King, Jr., and hands him a souvenir pen. (UNITED PRESS INTERNATIONAL)

More and more Americans heard Dr. King's ideas on nonviolent protest after the March on Washington. He spoke at civil rights rallies and from church pulpits all over the country. Some of the things Dr. King urged were to become the law of the land with the Civil Rights Act of 1964. The Civil Rights Act of 1964 opened parks, stadiums, swimming pools, and other public facilities to black people. Now, public accommodations such as restaurants, hotels, and gasoline stations were to be desegregated. When President Johnson signed the bill he said: "The Civil Rights Act is a challenge to all of us to go to work, in our homes and in our hearts, to eliminate the last vestiges of injustice in our beloved country. . . ."

Dr. Martin Luther King, Jr.,speaks at a civil rights rally in Chicago, June 21, 1964. (UNITED PRESS INTERNATIONAL)

In 1964, segregationists continued to threaten civil rights workers with violence. In St. Augustine, Florida, Dr. King examines the trunk lid of a car that has been covered with shotgun fire. The car belongs to a member of King's Southern Christian Leadership Conference. (UNITED PRESS INTERNATIONAL)

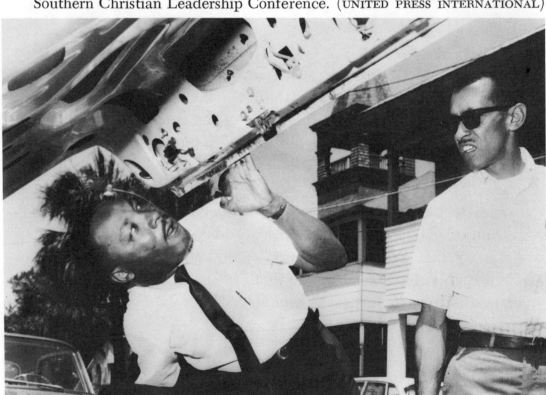

Dr. Martin Luther King, Jr., and the Reverend Ralph Abernathy were arrested during a sit-in at a motel restaurant in St. Augustine, Florida, in 1964. They were put in a cell in the St. John's County jail in St. Augustine. (UNITED PRESS INTERNATIONAL)

Dr. King was arrested and jailed thirty times during his civil rights career. In 1964, he was arrested in St. Augustine, Florida, for a sit-in demonstration. He shared his cell with the Reverend Ralph Abernathy, whom he jokingly called his perennial jail mate. Racists made a new attack on the civil rights movement in the summer of 1964, shortly after Dr. King was freed. That summer hundreds of young people from the Northeast had gone to Mississippi to work on a voter registration drive. Shortly after the campaign began, three civil rights workers disappeared. After a two-week search, Andrew Goodman, a student at Queens College in New York, Michael Schwerner, a New York social worker, and James E. Chaney, a black civil rights worker from Meridian, Mississippi, were found dead. Dr. King said that the triple murder would not put a stop to the struggle for black voter rights.

41

After a tour of Europe, Dr. King is received in audience by Pope Paul VI at the Vatican, on September 18. After the March on Washington, Dr. King was invited to speak to groups in several European countries. (UNITED PRESS INTERNATIONAL)

Dr. King consulted with more and more world leaders after the March on Washington. But he still had time for his followers, and especially for children. Here, Dr. King signs his autograph for a young girl before holding a press conference in St. Augustine, Florida, in August, 1964. (UNITED PRESS INTERNATIONAL)

Dr. Martin Luther King, Jr., his wife, and two of their four children are surrounded by reporters at the Atlanta, Georgia, airport. The Kings were on their way to Oslo, Norway, where the Nobel Peace Prize was to be awarded. The Nobel Peace Prize is the only Nobel prize to be awarded in Norway. The rest of the prizes are awarded in Stockholm where the Nobel foundation is located. (UNITED PRESS INTERNATIONAL)

THE NOBEL PEACE PRIZE

The Nobel Foundation in Stockholm, Sweden, in some years awards a Nobel Peace Prize to the man or woman who worked the hardest for peace and brotherhood in the world. In October, 1964, it was announced that that year's award would go to Dr. Martin Luther King, Jr., America's most famous civil rights leader since Booker T. Washington. Dr. King was the one hundred and fourteenth American and the youngest man to win the prize. He donated the cash award of $50,000, which accompanies the prize, to the civil rights movement. Dr. King felt that the prize was more than a personal honor. He believed that it gave honor to the entire civil rights struggle.

43

The attention of the world was on Dr. Martin Luther King, Jr., and on the cause for which he fought, when he received the Nobel Peace Prize from Gunnar Jahn, chairman of the Nobel Prize committee in Oslo, Norway, on December 10, 1964. (UNITED PRESS INTERNATIONAL)

Dr. Martin Luther King gives an acceptance speech after receiving the Nobel Peace Prize. (EBONY MAGAZINE)

The Nobel Peace Prize
(EBONY MAGAZINE)

Dr. King was honored with many citations and dinners when he returned from the Nobel Peace Prize awards in Norway. Here, King's daughter Yolanda tries to have a word with her mother and father at a testimonial dinner given in Dr. King's honor at an Atlanta hotel, in 1965. (UNITED PRESS INTERNATIONAL)

Dr. Martin Luther King, Jr., converses with Vice-President Hubert Humphrey at a dinner in New York in May, 1965. (UNITED PRESS INTERNATIONAL)

Dr. Martin Luther King stands with Dr. James Nabrit, Jr., president of Howard University, before delivering the principal speech at the University's Charter Day observance, March, 1965. (UNITED PRESS INTERNATIONAL)

Dr. King points to a map of Selma, Alabama, in his headquarters in Atlanta, Georgia, in 1965. Selma was to be the next scene of civil rights demonstrations. (UNITED PRESS INTERNATIONAL)

SELMA, ALABAMA, 1965

The Civil Rights Act of 1964 did not have firm guidelines on voting rights. In 1965 Dr. King believed that voting registration and school desegregation were the most important aims of the civil rights struggle. Only one percent of the voters of Selma, Alabama, with a population of 14,400 whites and 15,100 blacks, were black. Dr. King and his followers demonstrated in Selma in 1965 against unjust voter registration proceedings there. Selma's sheriff, James G. Clark, turned back hundreds of blacks that King led down to the county courthouse to register to vote. Many of these protesters were arrested. Over two thousand men, women, and children were jailed in demonstrations lasting over seven weeks. King himself was arrested and refused to post bond for four days.

Dr. Martin Luther King looks back at a long line of his followers in Selma, Alabama, in 1965. King and the demonstrators kneeled to pray after they had been arrested for marching for voter rights. (UNITED PRESS INTERNATIONAL)

In 1965, a federal marshal reads an injunction order prohibiting King's planned Selma-to-Montgomery voter rights march. Dr. King and the demonstrators began the march anyway, and they were arrested. (UNITED PRESS INTERNATIONAL)

In an effort to draw the nation's attention to Alabama's denial of voting rights to blacks, King organized a march from Selma, Alabama, to Montgomery, Alabama, the state capital. Alabama Governor George Wallace said that the march could not proceed as planned. But the demonstrators felt that they had the right to petition their government peacefully and decided to go ahead with the march. On March 7, 525 blacks, many of them with bedrolls and knapsacks, filed two abreast down the highway toward Montgomery. On U.S. Highway 80, 200 Alabama state troopers were ready to halt them. When the demonstrators did not retreat, the troopers started swinging their clubs. Bullwhips were lashed at those who fell, and in the chaos, tear gas was released. More then seventy-eight demonstrators had to be treated at a hospital. Protest marches in cities throughout the nation and in Canada were held to support the Selma campaign.

Civil rights marchers on their way from Selma to Montgomery are clubbed and gassed by Alabama state troopers. (CHARLES MOORE, BLACK STAR)

The march from Selma to Montgomery continues on March 17, 1965. The fifty-four-mile hike was made without incident. (STEVE SCHAPIRO, BLACK STAR)

Another attempt at the fifty-four-mile march from Selma to Montgomery was made on March 9, after President Johnson said the demonstrators had the right to march. Fifteen hundred black and white marchers were led by Dr. King. This march was also stopped — this time by a federal judge's order. Finally, on March 17, President Johnson sent the National Guard to protect the demonstrators along the route. Only 300 of the marchers were allowed on the road each day. But the rest of the demonstrators joined them in Montgomery on March 25, when the crowd numbered about 30,000. The march was marred by the death of three civil rights workers. Jimmie Lee Jackson, a young Negro marcher; the Reverend James Reeb, a minister from Boston; and Mrs. Viola Gregg Liuzzo, a Detroit housewife, had been killed by racists. After the Selma march, the Voting Rights Act of 1965 was passed by Congress. Dr. King was in the White House on August 6, when President Johnson signed the bill. The Voting Rights Act of 1965 abolished literacy tests and poll taxes, and provided federal registrars to register black citizens.

Dr. Martin Luther King, Jr., and his chief aide, the Reverend Ralph Abernathy, change socks during a roadside stop on the Selma-to-Montgomery march in 1965. (UNITED PRESS INTERNATIONAL)

Dr. King holds a press conference at the roadside on the way to Montgomery on the Selma-to-Montgomery march in 1965. (UNITED PRESS INTERNATIONAL)

Dr. Martin Luther King, Jr., and his wife lead the last part of the Selma-to-Montgomery civil rights march on March 25, 1965. The crowd numbered about 30,000 by the time the marchers reached the state capital. (UNITED PRESS INTERNATIONAL)

Entertainers Harry Belafonte (left) and Sammy Davis, Jr. (right), speak with Dr. Martin Luther King at a New York benefit show called "Broadway Answers Selma," in 1965. The benefit raised money for the Selma campaign. (UNITED PRESS INTERNATIONAL)

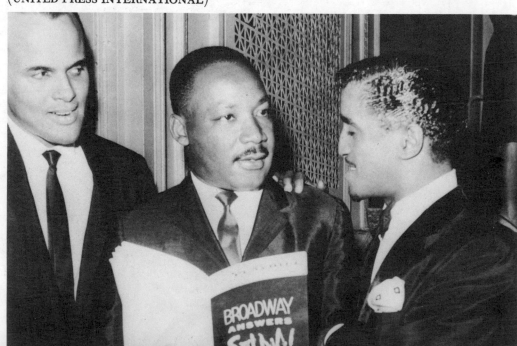

Leaders of the "Meredith March Against Fear," on June 26, 1966. Left to right: Dr. Martin Luther King, Jr., James Meredith, Stokely Carmichael, Floyd McKissick. (UNITED PRESS INTERNATIONAL)

BLACK POWER

On June 6, 1966, James Meredith, the student who integrated the University of Mississippi in 1962, took a solitary freedom walk from Memphis, Tennessee, to Jackson, Mississippi. He was shot on the way, but recovered shortly after. The march begun by Meredith was taken up again on June 7 by the civil rights groups. It was during this march that Stokely Carmichael, of the Student Nonviolent Coordinating Committee, turned the civil rights movement in a new direction. He coined the slogan "Black Power." The three big civil rights leaders walked arm in arm in the march, but the gulf between Dr. King and the other two leaders was growing. Floyd McKissick, national director of the Congress of Racial Equality, said that nonviolence had become a dead philosophy. King's greatest test had begun. He believed in black awareness and black pride, but he was against the idea of black supremacy and violence. He said that "If every Negro in America turns to violence, I'll still stand against it." Some of his followers were no longer willing to stand with him.

53

One black leader who did not follow Dr. King's philosophy was Elijah Muhammad, head of the Black Muslim movement. Elijah Muhammad preached the separation of the races and a philosophy of black nationalism. (UNITED PRESS INTERNATIONAL)

Malcolm X, a disciple of Elijah Muhammad, holds up *Muhammad Speaks*, the newspaper of the Black Muslim movement in 1963. Malcolm X, who was becoming more and more popular with many black people, and particularly young militants, broke with the Black Muslims later that year. He was assassinated while speaking in the Audubon Ballroom in Harlem, on February 21, 1965. Three black men were accused of the murder. (WIDE WORLD PHOTOS)

Dr. Martin Luther King, Jr., speaks to a group of residents from Watts, Los Angeles, after the six-day riot in 1965. Dr. King was heckled by many who felt he was not in touch with their problems. (UNITED PRESS INTERNATIONAL)

NORTHERN GHETTOS

The Watts section of Los Angeles, a black ghetto, was the scene of a six-day riot of burning and looting in August, 1965. The riot brought attention to the frustration and despair of the Northern urban black man. In the North, segregation and discrimination were less open than in the South, but they were there nevertheless. Ghetto life, poverty, unemployment, inadequate housing, and welfare were problems that Dr. King had neglected while he worked to integrate public facilities in the South. He realized now that the problems of racism were nationwide. He said, "What good does it do to be able to eat at a lunch counter if you can't buy a hamburger." Dr. King toured Northern cities to try to turn ghetto despair into nonviolent action. But more and more young black people questioned his philosophy.

Dr. King went to Chicago, Illinois, in 1966, to fight for an end to discrimination in housing, schools, and employment. He addressed a crowd of 45,000 blacks at Soldier Field on July 10. Later he went to Chicago's city hall where he taped a list of demands on the door. On July 29 Dr. King began a campaign for open housing in an all-white community in the southwest section of the city. Whites gathered by the side of the road and threw rocks and bottles at the demonstrators. Dr. King was hit on the head with a rock thrown by angry white residents of the Gage Park section of the city, on August 5, when he led six hundred demonstrators on another open housing march.

Dr. Martin Luther King, with shovel in hand, helps clean up an alley in Chicago, in 1966. He came to the city to press for open housing and slum clearance. (DONALD M. SCHWARTZ)

Dr. Martin Luther King was hit on the head by a rock as he led a protest march against housing discrimination in an all-white Chicago neighborhood on August 5, 1966. (UNITED PRESS INTERNATIONAL)

Dr. Martin Luther King leads civil rights marchers through driving rain in an open housing demonstration in an all-white neighborhood in South Deering, Michigan, on August 21, 1966. (UNITED PRESS INTERNATIONAL)

THE VIETNAM WAR

His strong belief in civil rights and nonviolence made Dr. King one of the leading opponents of American participation in the war in Vietnam. When President Johnson first took office, he had said that the United States would go to war on poverty, and would attempt to end ghettos, slum housing, and unemployment. However, the war in Vietnam was consuming billions of dollars a year. Dr. King felt that the war was unjust and was diverting badly needed funds from the poor in America. King was loudly criticized by some white and Negro leaders for his position on the Vietnam War. But King continued to draw attention to the fact that poverty existed in America, and that something must be done about it. He decided to organize another large biracial march on Washington to dramatize the problems of the poor and to stir Congress to legislative action. He called his campaign the Poor People's Campaign.

Dr. Martin Luther King, Jr., speaking at a peace rally in front of the United Nations Plaza in New York on April 15, 1967. (UNITED PRESS INTERNATIONAL)

Dr. Benjamin Spock, a baby doctor who spoke out against the war in Vietnam, and Dr. Martin Luther King, Jr., lead marchers through Chicago in protest against the war in Vietnam on March 25, 1967. (UNITED PRESS INTERNATIONAL)

Dr. Martin Luther King embraces a nine-year-old girl as he is greeted by schoolchildren at Mount Calvary Baptist Church in Newark, New Jersey. In 1968 King toured Newark to ask for support for his upcoming Poor People's Campaign. (UNITED PRESS INTERNATIONAL)

Dr. Martin Luther King is surrounded by leaders of the Memphis sanitation strike on March 28, 1968, as he arrives to lead a march. (UNITED PRESS INTERNATIONAL)

MEMPHIS, TENNESSEE

Dr. King's attention was diverted from plans for the Poor People's Campaign, in March, 1968, by a sanitation strike in Memphis, Tennessee. Thirteen hundred sanitation workers, most of whom were black, had been striking for better wages since February. Dr. King believed that the strike was representative of the problems of poverty that he was trying to deal with in his campaign, and he went to Memphis to lead a march in behalf of the strikers. The first march was a great disappointment to him. Most of the marchers remained nonviolent, but some youths began to loot stores and break windows. This was the first time in Dr. King's long history of civil rights activities that one of his marches had broken out into violence. His philosophy was being rejected by his own people, and this depressed and discouraged him. He wanted to try again, and he began to plan another march.

Broken windows and looters on a downtown Memphis street following the march led by Dr. Martin Luther King on March 28, 1968. (UNITED PRESS INTERNATIONAL)

National Guardsmen in Memphis with fixed bayonets and armored personnel block Beale Street, the scene of looting and rioting the day before. Demonstrators walk past the guardsmen. (UNITED PRESS INTERNATIONAL)

ASSASSINATION

The threat of death had always loomed over Dr. King and his family. They had become used to menacing telephone calls and letters. Dr. King's flight to Memphis had been delayed while airline officials searched passengers' baggage for a bomb that an anonymous caller said had been placed on the plane. On April 3, King spoke to two thousand cheering supporters. He challenged America to defeat racism and poverty. In a prophetic speech he said, "We've got some difficult days ahead. But it really doesn't matter with me now. Because I've been to the mountaintop. I won't mind. Like anybody I would like to live a long life . . . but I'm not concerned with that now, I just want to do God's will. I may not get there with you, but I want you to know tonight that we as a people will get to the promised land."

Dr. Martin Luther King, Jr., was shot as he stood on the balcony of this Memphis motel on April 4, 1968. (UNITED PRESS INTERNATIONAL)

The widow of Dr. Martin Luther King, the slain civil rights leader, leads a memorial march on April 8. In front row, left to right: singer Harry Belafonte; King's daughter Yolanda; sons, Martin III and Dexter; Mrs. Coretta King; the Reverend Ralph Abernathy; and the Reverend Andrew Young. Ten thousand people joined Mrs. King in the memorial march. (UNITED PRESS INTERNATIONAL)

On Thursday evening, April 4, 1968, Dr. Martin Luther King, Jr., was killed by a single bullet that came crashing into his neck as he stood on the balcony of the Lorraine Motel in Memphis. He had been chatting minutes earlier with some friends. Dr. King died about an hour later despite emergency surgery at St. Joseph's Hospital. Mrs. King, who had been informed that her husband had been shot, learned of his death at the Atlanta airport where she was waiting for a plane to Memphis. The tragedy shocked the nation and the world. The Nobel Prize-winning civil rights leader was dead. A great spokesman for peace and nonviolence had been struck down. President Johnson proclaimed Sunday, April 7, a national day of mourning for Dr. King. A memorial march was led by Mrs. King on Monday, April 8, in Memphis.

A staff member of the Southern Christian Leadership Conference gathers cards accompanying floral tributes to Dr. Martin Luther King. He is standing at the spot where the civil rights leader was struck down. (UNITED PRESS INTERNATIONAL)

Hundreds of marchers enter New York's Central Park on April 7 in tribute to the late Dr. Martin Luther King, Jr. (UNITED PRESS INTERNATIONAL)

Mule-drawn caisson carries the casket of Dr. Martin Luther King, Jr., toward the campus of Morehouse College for a memorial service. Dignitaries and friends of Dr. King followed the caisson to the service. (UNITED PRESS INTERNATIONAL)

An aerial view shows the winding line of people who came to the campus of Spelman College to view the body of slain civil rights leader Dr. Martin Luther King, Jr., in the Sisters Chapel (columned building in center). (UNITED PRESS INTERNATIONAL)

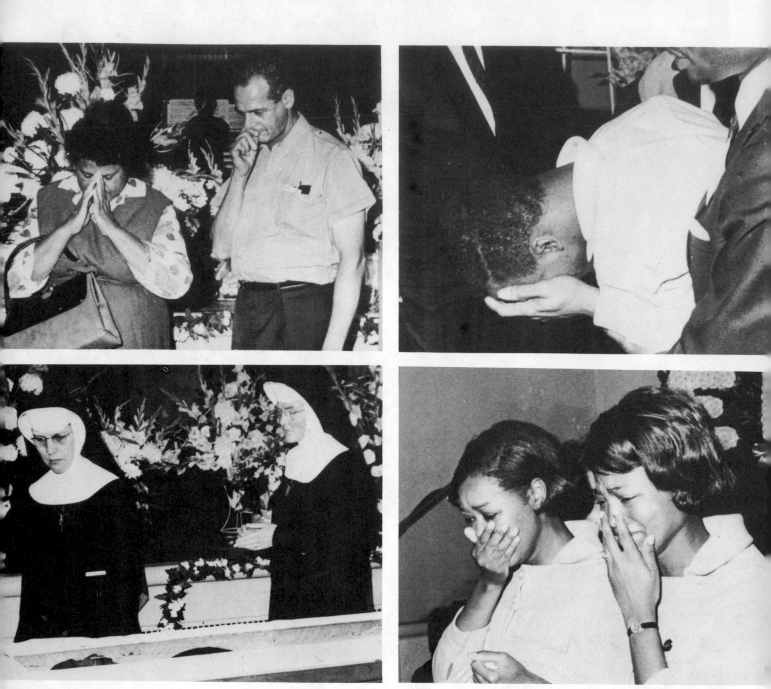

The grief of his followers is mirrored in their faces as they come to view the body of slain civil rights leader Dr. Martin Luther King, Jr., lying in state at the Sisters Chapel of Spelman College in Atlanta, Georgia. (UNITED PRESS INTERNATIONAL)

Dr. Martin Luther King, Jr., was buried at South View Cemetery in Atlanta, Georgia, where other members of the King family are interred. (UNITED PRESS INTERNATIONAL)

Dr. Martin Luther King, Jr., a prophet of peace and America's foremost leader of the nonviolent civil rights movement, was dead at the age of thirty-nine. He had been courageous in the totality of his commitment to nonviolence. He was caught between the anger of black militants who preached a more aggressive position and white extremists who could not stand to see any change at all. He faced insult and danger constantly. It is ironic that a man so devoted to peace should have been followed so often by the very violence he was trying so hard to defeat. But Dr. King's outcry for justice *was* dramatized to the world, and to many he was the Moses of his people.

THE WORDS OF MARTIN LUTHER KING, JR.

"If we are arrested every day, if we are exploited every day, if we are trampled over every day, don't ever let anyone pull you so low as to hate them. We must use the weapon of love. We must have compassion and understanding for those who hate us. We must realize so many people are taught to hate us that they are not totally responsible for their hate. But we stand in life at midnight; we are always on the threshold of a new dawn."

MARTIN LUTHER KING, JR.

"I say to you today, my friends, that in spite of the difficulties and frustrations of the moment I still have a dream. It is a dream deeply rooted in the American dream.

I have a dream that one day this nation will rise up and live out the true meaning of its creed: 'We hold these truths to be self-evident; that all men are created equal.'

I have a dream that one day on the red hills of Georgia the sons of former slaves and the sons of former slaveowners will be able to sit down together at the table of brotherhood.

I have a dream that one day even the state of Mississippi, a desert state sweltering with the heat of injustice and oppression, will be transformed into an oasis of freedom and justice.

I have a dream that my four little children will one day live in a nation where they will not be judged by the color of their skin but by the content of their character."

An excerpt from the "I Have a Dream" speech.

MARTIN LUTHER KING, JR.

INDEX